MATH ON MY PATH

Math at the LIBRARY

Elise Craver

Rourke Educational Media
A Division of Carson Dellosa Education

ROURKE'S **SCHOOL to HOME** CONNECTIONS

BEFORE AND DURING READING ACTIVITIES

Before Reading: *Building Background Knowledge and Vocabulary*

Building background knowledge can help children process new information and build upon what they already know. Before reading a book, it is important to tap into what children already know about the topic. This will help them develop their vocabulary and increase their reading comprehension.

Questions and Activities to Build Background Knowledge:

1. Look at the front cover of the book and read the title. What do you think this book will be about?
2. What do you already know about this topic?
3. Take a book walk and skim the pages. Look at the table of contents, photographs, captions, and bold words. Did these text features give you any information or predictions about what you will read in this book?

Vocabulary: *Vocabulary Is Key to Reading Comprehension*

Use the following directions to prompt a conversation about each word.

- Read the vocabulary words.
- What comes to mind when you see each word?
- What do you think each word means?

Vocabulary Words:

- *estimate*
- *pentagon*
- *unit*
- *weigh*

During Reading: *Reading for Meaning and Understanding*

To achieve deep comprehension of a book, children are encouraged to use close reading strategies. During reading, it is important to have children stop and make connections. These connections result in deeper analysis and understanding of a book.

Close Reading a Text

During reading, have children stop and talk about the following:

- Any confusing parts
- Any unknown words
- Text to text, text to self, text to world connections
- The main idea in each chapter or heading

Encourage children to use context clues to determine the meaning of any unknown words. These strategies will help children learn to analyze the text more thoroughly as they read.

When you are finished reading this book, turn to the last page for an **After Reading Activity**.

Table of Contents

Math Is All Around

We can find many books at a library.

Some libraries also have computers and other tools.

But did you know a library has math too?

Numbers at the Library

Books with numbers on their covers go together in a set.

What do you notice about these two sets?

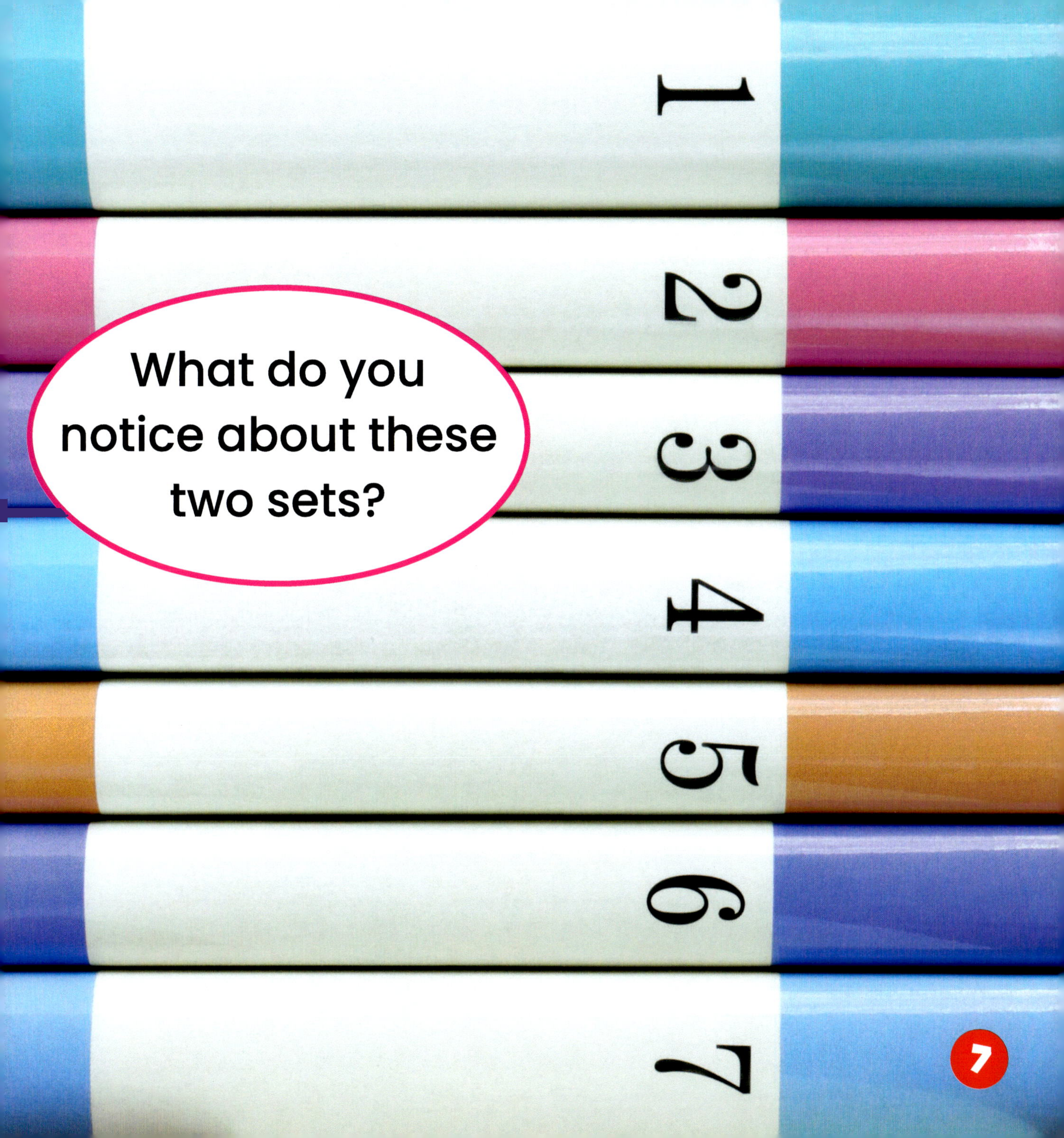

The librarian is working hard. What is she doing with these books?

How can numbers help describe what you see?

It’s story time!

Are there more boys or girls listening?

What else do you notice?

About how many books do you think are on one shelf?

How did you **estimate**?

DER EINZIGE ORT
HEATH
ALLES AUF ANFANG
Hit Refresh | Satya Nadella
BELTRACCHI
100 JAHRE LYRIK
BESTOFBESTWOMEN·SEROTICA
BRAUNSTEIN · PÉPIN
1 Kilo KULTUR
C.H.BECK
THEA DORN RICHARD WAGNER
Die deutsche Seele
ZITATE
HANS-HORST SKUPY
Orbis
DANIEL GALERA
Ernst Trost Prinz Eugen
2018 JAHRBUCH RECHTE GEWALT
KNAUR
Die ganze Wahrheit über Gluten
SMART CAPITALISM
Samuel Shem
DOCTOR FINE
Good Life
campus
ROBINSON CRUSOE
Daniel Defoe
MARY BEARD
SPQR
REVOLUTION DANK INNOVATION
THORSTEN REITER
Kongreß ohne Streß
Facebook Gesellschaft
José Díaz Herrera e Isabel Durán
El saqueo de España
EINFACH erfolgreich anlegen
VOLKES STIMMEN
Das Joseph Conrad Buch
JANE GOODALL
REASON FOR HOPE
Rudolf Leonhard
IN DERSELBEN NACHT
Gesundheit aus eigener Kraft
HENRIK MÜLLER DIE SIEBEN KNAPPHEITEN
campus
ALLES KUNST?
Kursbuch 77
1984
WENN DU NICHT MEHR BRENNST, STARTE NEU
REFORMATION DES HERZENS
Womit ich nie gerechnet habe
Götz W. Werner
Econ
DVA
HANDWERK

Measuring at the Library

Check out the stack of books she is holding! Books can be heavy.

He is holding a book too. Does it **weigh** more or less than the books he is sitting on?

He is standing on tiptoe to reach a book.

How tall do you think that bookcase is?

What **unit**
would you use
to measure it?

Shapes at the Library

There are many different kinds of books.

What shapes and sizes do you see here?

These computers help people find information.

What shapes do you notice in the computer area?

Here is a mini library!

Each section is a **pentagon**.

What other shapes do you see?

STÍN KONDORA

Photo Glossary

estimate (ES-tuh-mate): To use what you know to make a smart guess about how many or how much.

pentagon (PEN-tuh-gahn): A flat two-dimensional shape with five sides and five corners.

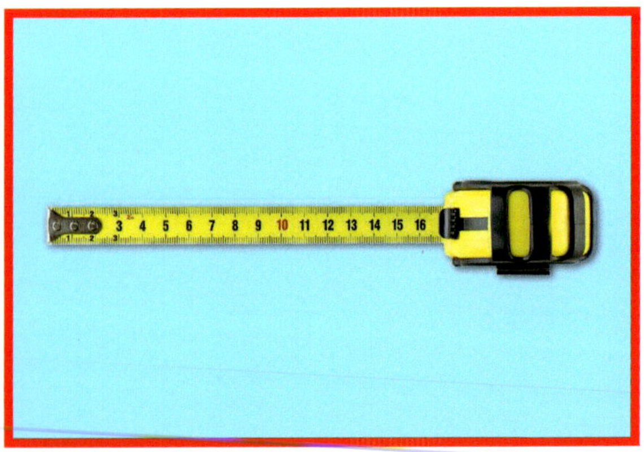

unit (YOO-nit): An amount used as a standard measurement.

weigh (way): To have an amount of heaviness.

Activity: Book Olympics

Compare and rank a group of books to figure out which is the biggest, the heaviest, the longest, and more!

Supplies

scissors
gold-colored paper
markers
ruler or paper clips
scale
five different books
paper
pencil
tape

Directions

1. Cut circles from gold paper. Use markers to decorate and label one "medal" for each category you will be measuring—tallest, heaviest, longest, etc.
2. For each category, use the correct tool to measure each book. Record the results on a separate sheet of paper. If you are just starting to learn how to measure, line up paper clips to measure with instead of using a ruler.
3. Write the name of each winner on the matching medal and tape it to the front of the book.
4. Share your final rankings with a friend. Explain how you determined the winner of each category and anything surprising you noticed.

Index

About the Author

Elise Craver is a former teacher who lives in North Carolina. She loves to discover new books and authors at her local library. She didn't like math as a kid but loves it now. She and her two kids are always looking for math problems in real life.

After Reading Activity

Take a trip to a nearby library and play library math I Spy. Use math terms to describe something you see in the library and challenge a friend to figure out what it is. For example, say, "I spy something far away," or "I spy an even number."

Library of Congress PCN Data

Math at the Library / Elise Craver
(Math on My Path)
ISBN 978-1-73163-839-7 (hard cover)(alk. paper)
ISBN 978-1-73163-916-5 (soft cover)
ISBN 978-1-73163-993-6 (e-Book)
ISBN 978-1-73164-070-3 (ePub)
Library of Congress Control Number: 2020930194

Rourke Educational Media
Printed in the United States of America
08-1252511937

www.rourkeeducationalmedia.com

Edited by: Hailey Scragg
Cover design by: Rhea Magaro-Wallace, Lynne Schwaner
Interior design by: Kathy Walsh, Alison Tracey
Photo Credits: Cover, p 1 ©urfinguss; p 5 ©Kzenon; p 6 ©herpens; p 7 ©Mauro Carli; p 8, 9 ©DusanManic; p 10, 11, 15 ©FatCamera; p 12, 13, 22 ©clu; p 14, 22 ©SDI Productions; p 16, 17 ©diignat; p 16, 22 ©Roman Valiev; p 18 ©Johnathan21; p 19 ©Rawpixel.com; p 20, 21, 22 ©rdonar